Disability PRIDE

Having a Voice Matters

Jeni Vasquez

PowerKiDS press

Published in 2026 by The Rosen Publishing Group, Inc.
2544 Clinton Street, Buffalo, NY 14224

First Edition

Editor: Danielle Haynes
Book Design: Leslie Taylor

Photo Credits: Cover, p. 5 fizkes/Shutterstock.com; (series background) P.siripak/Shutterstock.com; (series disability pride colors) rudall30/Shutterstock.com; p. 5 (flag sidebar) Maxim Studio/Shutterstock.com; p. 7 PeopleImages.com - Yuri A/Shutterstock.com; p. 9 Daisy Daisy/Shutterstock.com; p. 11 SofikoS/Shutterstock.com; p. 13 Media_Photos/Shutterstock.com; p. 15 National Museum of American History Smithsonian Institution/File:Photo of President George H. W. Bush signing the Americans with Disabilities Act inscribed to Justin Dart, Jr., 1990.jpg_commons.wikimedia.com; p. 17 courtesy of Dorian Bonner, City of Long Beach/X.com; pp. 19, 21 wavebreakmedia/Shutterstock.com.

Library of Congress Cataloging-in-Publication Data

Names: Vasquez, Jeni author
Title: Having a voice matters / Jeni Vasquez.
Description: Buffalo : PowerKids Press, [2026] | Series: Disability pride | Includes bibliographical references and index.
Identifiers: LCCN 2025031629 | ISBN 9781499456981 library binding | ISBN 9781499456974 paperback | ISBN 9781499456998 ebook
Subjects: LCSH: People with disabilities–Juvenile literature | Discrimination against people with disabilities–Juvenile literature | Disabilities–Juvenile literature | Activism–Juvenile literature
Classification: LCC HV1568 .V377 2026
LC record available at https://lccn.loc.gov/2025031629

Manufactured in the United States of America

Some of the images in this book illustrate individuals who are models. The depictions do not imply actual situations or events.

CPSIA Compliance Information: Batch #CWPK26. For Further Information contact Rosen Publishing at 1-800-237-9932.

Contents

Different Voices

Using your voice can mean different things. It can mean a voice you create with your mouth and throat using words. It also can mean **communication** with sign language or a computer or in writing. In all these ways, it means to **express** yourself. It's important to communicate about your own experiences and stories and tell others your thoughts and feelings.

Everyone with a disability has a different journey. It can be important for you to share yours! And for those without a disability, using your voice to boost, or lift, your friends' voices can be a great way to be an **ally**.

The disability pride flag was created to show acceptance and respect for people who have disabilities. Each color is for a different type of disability.

- The gray background is in honor of those who've died.
- Green is for disabilities that have to do with the senses.
- Blue is for those that have to do with the mind and emotions.
- White stands for unseen disabilities as well as those that haven't been diagnosed, or found out.
- Gold is for neurodiversity.
- Red is for other disabilities of the body.

There are many ways to have a voice. No matter which ones you use, your voice is important!

What Is a Disability?

A disability can be many different things. Generally, it's a **physical** or **mental** issue that can make it harder to do certain things and **interact** with the world. A disability can affect someone's senses or how they can move. It can affect how they learn or think or communicate.

Sometimes you can see if someone has a disability. They might use a wheelchair or another tool to help them. They might need to communicate in a different way. Sometimes, though, a disability can be invisible. This means you can't see it. This doesn't make it any less real.

Invisible disabilities can include learning disorders, mental illnesses, and disorders such as asthma, or trouble breathing.

Learn More

Sometimes, people have a disability from birth. Sometimes, it's something that starts later in their life or is related to an injury or a condition.

Diversity Within Disability

People can have more than one disability, and even within types of disabilities, things can be different. Don't **assume** that everyone is the same! Everyone has different wants and needs and abilities. For example, if you have autism and prefer to do things a certain way, it doesn't mean that a classmate with autism will want the same things. People with disabilities are very **diverse**, and disabilities themselves can be very diverse.

This is important to remember when you use your voice to speak up about disabilities. You shouldn't assume everyone wants the same things!

People with autism may use tools such as headphones or fidget items to help them deal with issues at school.

Learn More

"Neurodiversity" is a word that means the different ways that people's brains work. It often applies to autism, attention-deficit/hyperactivity disorder (ADHD), and learning differences.

A Long History

It's important to know you can speak up about your rights. In the United States, there's a long history of people talking about disability pride and disability rights! At one point, many people didn't support those with disabilities in many ways. They didn't always think they had an equal right to things other people had, such as **access** to housing, jobs, and other basic human rights.

In the 20th century, more people started using their voices to call for these rights. The Americans with Disabilities Act (ADA) became law in 1990. The ADA makes it against the law to **discriminate** against people because of disabilities.

The ADA applies to people of all ages, both kids and adults!

Speaking Up

You can understand why it's important to use your voice to speak up for disability rights. However, it's also important to pay attention to what you're saying! If you have a disability and want to talk about it, that's great. It's good for other people to understand your life and what is and isn't helpful to you.

But be careful if you're talking about something you don't fully understand. Your experience with your disability might be different from that of other people. What's helpful to you might not be helpful to them. And people with a different disability may have another experience altogether.

Learn More

There's a difference between equality and equity. Equality means everyone gets the same **resources**. Equity means they get the resources they need based on that need.

People might not want to talk about their disabilities. It's important to respect that too!

Historic Speakers

So, how do you use your voice? People throughout history have done so to talk about disability rights. Justin Dart Jr. was one of these speakers. Dart had an illness called polio when he was a teenager. After that, he had to use a wheelchair. He became a businessman who worked to support the rights of those with disabilities.

During the 1980s, Dart traveled to all 50 U.S. states to talk to other people with disabilities and speak out in support of the Americans with Disabilities Act. Dart continued to work for people's rights until he died in 2002. He's remembered as the "godfather of the ADA."

When President George H. W. Bush signed the ADA in 1990, Dart was one of the people there. He's the one wearing the hat, on the right.

Learn More

President Bill Clinton honored Dart with the Presidential Medal of Freedom in 1998.

Young people speak up for the rights of those with disabilities too. Helena Donato-Sapp is one of these **activists**. She has several learning disabilities, including ADHD and dyscalculia. She encountered bullying and **ableism** in school but chose to speak up about her pride in her **identity**, including her disabilities.

As of 2025, Donato-Sapp is a teenager who works with the National Education Association (NEA). She has been a speaker at NEA conferences and has presented to many organizations about social justice and her experiences and goals. She's also a poet, artist, and writer.

Learn More

Dyscalculia is a learning disorder in which people struggle when dealing with math and numbers.

Helena Donato-Sapp speaks at a Black History Month celebration in Long Beach, California.

Be a Good Ally

Even if you don't have a disability yourself, you can be an ally to people with disabilities. However, it's important to be a *good* ally. This means you listen first! Don't assume you know what people with disabilities need. Listen when they tell you what helps and what hurts. However, you do need to learn on your own as well and not just expect people to educate you about disabilities.

It's good to speak up if you see a problem. It can be even better to lift the voices of people with disabilities when they say there's a problem.

Learn More

It's important to use the right language when talking about disabilities. Not everyone likes the same ways of speaking about disability. Again, listening is key!

If someone tells you they don't like how you speak about their disability, you don't argue. You just stop doing it!

Use Your Voice

So, you've learned about disabilities (not just your own) and you're ready to speak up. How can you use your voice? It can be as simple as saying something to a teacher about an accessibility issue in the classroom. It could be telling a classmate that their word choices about disability are harmful. It's important to say something instead of just looking away.

Maybe you'll want or need to do more. You could speak or write to the school board if there's a bigger accessibility issue. You could go to an event in which many people speak up for disability rights. Your voice matters!

Glossary

ableism: To discriminate against someone with a disability.

access: The ability to use or enter something.

activist: Someone who acts strongly in support of or against an issue.

ally: A person associated with another for support or a common purpose.

assume: To take something as granted or true.

communication: The use of words, sounds, signs, or behaviors to convey ideas, thoughts, and feelings.

discriminate: To treat people unequally based on ability, class, race, or religion.

diverse: Having many different types, forms, or ideas.

express: To communicate what you're thinking or feeling.

identity: The qualities, beliefs, etc., that make a particular person or group different from others.

interact: To come together and have an effect on each other.

mental: Of or relating to the mind.

physical: Relating to the body instead of the mind.

resource: Something that can be used.

For More Information

BOOKS

Cocca-Leffler, Maryann, and Janine Leffler. *We Want to Go to School! The Fight for Disability Rights.* Chicago, IL: Albert Whitman & Company, 2021.

Klatte, Kathleen A. *What Happens When I Have to Use a Wheelchair?* Buffalo, NY: Powerkids Press, 2025.

Paul, Miranda. *Right Now! Real Kids Speaking Up for Change.* Boston, MA: Clarion Books, 2021.

WEBSITES

Junior Scholastic: The Fight for Disability Rights
www.junior.scholastic.com/pages/promotion/031521/the-fight-for-disability-rights.html
Junior Scholastic showcases a look at the path of disability rights in the United States.

Helena
www.helenalourdes.com
Learn more about activist Helena Donato-Sapp on her website.

NEA: Words Matter!
www.nea.org/words-matter-disability-language-etiquette
The National Education Association provides a look at language about disability.

Publisher's note to educators and parents: Our editors have carefully reviewed these websites to ensure that they are suitable for students. Many websites change frequently, however, and we cannot guarantee that a site's future contents will continue to meet our high standards of quality and educational value. Be advised that students should be closely supervised whenever they access the internet.

Index